A Collection of Nightmares

Xia Laniel

Presentation by *BookLeaf Publishing*

Web: www.bookleafpub.com

E-mail: info@bookleafpub.com

ISBN: 9789395756228

First edition 2022

DEDICATION

This book is dedicated to my three naughty children, who always find ways to keep my life exciting, my biggest fan, supporter, and cheerleader, Annette, and to all my fellow horror fanatics.

You Are Here

I emerged, dizzy and confused.
My face felt wet, my eye stayed shut;
The earth felt damp under my hands as I lifted
myself up.
Where are we?
How did we get here?

I tried to pull away, my legs wouldn't budge.
Strange smells permeated the air; what were
those smells?
Gasoline, maybe?
Maybe a hint of pine under the stench of my
own..
Blood?

The light was bright.
So bright, it blinded me.
But then,
I saw a hand.
I extended my own, reached as far as I could,
but it just wasn't far enough.
It started getting hot; why did it get hot?

A high pitched ringing tore through my ears.
There was a whisper of a voice underneath.

I tried to listen, but there was only constant
screaming.
What were you saying?
Were you calling my name?

I called out, but there was no sound.
The faint whisper came again, if only I could've
made it out.
I reached again, for the disembodied hand,
and pulled with everything I had.
An arm, a face, a torso, it was you.

I started getting cold; where did the heat go?
It was so unbearable the minute before.
I heard the whisper again, it was calling my
name.
Then, the light consumed me, and all went cold.
All went black.

Here I stand, and now I see.
You were here.
Our mangled car wrapped 'round the tree.
The fire, your hand reaching out for me;
"The gasoline!"
I'm pulling you, you're pulling me.
You stayed behind, and I was freed.
In the charred abyss,
I fall to my knees and scream.

Underneath sobs, footsteps approach.
I can't hardly speak with this frog in my throat.
The sound is familiar as the steps are drawing
near,
then I hear your voice saying,
"I know you are here."

My Sunshine

6:59 am.
The radio clicks on:

"You are my sunshine, my only sunshine..."

I stir and rub my eyes, I have to turn the radio
off.
That damn song; my eyes well up with tears.
Not today; please, not today.
The hole in my chest starts to open as I slam my
hand on the clock.
Anything to make it go away.

As I try to continue on with my day,
the mirror swings the other way;
"I already told you, not today."
Another click:
"You make me happy, when skies are grey..."
The hole in my chest starts to deepen,
and for a moment,
I stood there weeping.

Later this evening, as I lay sleeping,
a force beckons me to awake.

3:33 am.
The click again:
"You'll never know dear, how much I love
you..."

I open my eyes, and to my surprise,
your loving face smiling back at me.

I've missed you so much,
hold me and never let me go.
I wrap my arms around you;
there's so much you need to know.
I close my eyes, grip you tight,
bury my head in your neck,
and take a deep breath.

I open my eyes, and to my surprise,
a dark, empty bedroom stares back at me.
My arms, still holding where you were;
the tears again, everything blurs.
"Please don't take my sunshine away..."
is all I can say;
the hole in my chest expands,
and consumes me.

Then, the sound of my alarm.

I bolt up-right, was it only a dream?
It is the morning; it was only a nightmare,

it seems.

Click

"The other night dear, as I lay sleeping..."
My blood runs cold.

"I dreamt I held you, in my arms..."
"Please stop," I say as the tears stream down my
face.

"When I awoke dear, I was mistaken..."
I curl up into a ball and hold my head.
My eyes are swelling, I can't see anything.
There's the hole again, I can feel it expanding
from within.

"So I hung my head, and cried..."

My throat tightens,
"You are my sunshine..."

Waterworld

Dead silent, no one around;
this is my favorite time to use the pool.
I relish in the stillness, then take a deep, heavy
breath.
Let the ritual begin.

I peel my layers of clothing off
until there's nothing left but my swimsuit;
everything piled neatly next to my bag and
towel.
One foot in front of the other,
I approach the side of the pool.
I take another chlorine scented breath,
and take a moment to watch the reflections in
the surface.
In this moment, all thought and time disappear.

I raise my arms above me, one hand neatly over
the other.

One more breath.

I allow my body to fall forward, hands leading
the way.

I can feel the water as it touches every inch of
my body,
like a wet, weightless hug.
The first dive is always the best;
for a moment, I hang suspended,
the water cradling and supporting me in this
space.
These are the true moments of peace,
this is my Zero Point.
Where all things are weightless, effortless,
where nothing else exists,
simply suspended in the present moment.

I move for the first time after entering the water,
first one arm, then the other.
My legs follow suit.
I keep going until my hand hits the wall,
and I rise to the surface.
A few breaths later, I dive in again,
making my way back to the other side.

Back and forth,
hanging and suspending as before.
A few breaths again, and back to the other side.
I swim and swim, yet my hands hit nothing.
"Maybe I'm getting tired, and it's taking longer."
I swim and swim, until I have to surface,
I can no longer take it.
Once above, I open my eyes;

I'm next to the wall, right where I started.
"Hmm.. maybe I swam down instead of across?"
I tell myself, my gut says otherwise.

A few more breaths, and across again.
I know for sure now,
exactly what I'm doing.
I swim and swim, and still I hit nothing.
I push myself faster,
yet it doesn't matter.
I breach the surface and see once again,
I am where I was before.

Frustrated, I climb out of the pool.
I slick the water off of my body,
and flick it on the ground.
"I'm going to jump in this time;
there's no way I won't reach the other side."
I run and jump, body following my hands,
into the water again.

I swim and swim, determined to hit something.
I push myself harder,
"The wall is coming."
And still, nothing.

I rise above again, I'm in the middle this time.
"At least it's something."
I breathe, treading.

A few breaths go by,
and then,
something slithers up my foot,
and around my ankle.
I kick and thrash, but it does nothing;
I am pulled under.

Deeper and deeper,
still kicking and thrashing.
I feel my chest tightening,
my ears popping,
and suddenly, it lets go.
I swim frantically to get to the surface.
As I get closer, I swear I can hear something.
Are those voices?
It seems like they're yelling;
a loud boom sounds,
and I feel the shockwave in the water.

I breach the surface a final time;
no pool, no walls.
"What the hell?"
Only endless ocean, pieces of a wreckage,
a galleon not far from me;
the air is heavy with gunpowder.
"We got a flo'ah,"
a grisly voice announces,
the galleon approaches.
A rope ladder falls from above,

and I make my way up.

At the top, I'm greeted with pointed blades,
and half-rotted faces.
"Well, would'ya look at the face of 'hat one?
What d'ya think, Cap'n?"

The ship falls silent as footsteps approach,
the crew makes way and parts like the sea.
Thump, thump, thump.
A tall, peg-legged man approaches,
much taller than the rest,
he smells of rot, of fish, and death.
His blind eyes stare right into mine,
his flesh hanging off his half-skeleton face.
I know now, there is no escape.
"Welcome to the Flying Dutchman;
we've been waiting for you, mate."

Sleep Tight

Slowly, I open my eyes,
and turn to shut off my alarm.
I know I have to get up,
but my bed is just so soft and warm.
Just 5 more minutes?
The bed entices me;
I lay back down, and drift back to sleep.

How long has it been?
Still drowsy again,
I can barely lift my head off my pillow,
my bones feel heavy.
How am I even more exhausted?
3 hours have gone by since I last fell asleep.

With only sheer will,
I sit upright, and rub my eyes.
I have to get up, I have plans today.
Still, I'm reluctant.
I stretch my body,
head towards the foot of my bed,
an arm out in front of me.
And plop onto the bed,
and lay in this pose.
Before too long, I drift and I snooze.

Mmm, I struggle to move.
The sheets are a bit tight this time;
have I tangled myself in the blankets?
I try to pull my arms from under the covers,
and struggle.
Are they getting tighter?
Now I have to get out.
I wiggle and squirm,
trying to slide my way out,
when suddenly,
the bed snaps in half and closes in on itself,
swallowing me whole.

The walls start closing in, the sheets are getting
tighter.
I struggle, but to no avail,
it's embrace is crushing me.
I take my last breath as my ribs snap and
collapse.

Goodnight, sleep tight.
Don't let the bed...
bite.

Dermatillomania

Spots, everywhere are spots.
Pimples, blackheads, whiteheads,
in-grown hairs;
on my face, on my neck, my shoulders,
arms, legs..

So many spots,
so many imperfections.
I have to get them out.
I start pinching and squeezing.
Even the smallest of spots has to go.
I am satisfied watching the contents pop out.
The imperfections are removed.

What's this?
A spot on my face;
I squeeze and squeeze, yet nothing comes out.
I try again, I know for certain there's something
there.
And I can't get it out, and it needs to come out.
I squeeze more, the skin ruptures,
and plasma oozes out.
I can see a yellowish ball beneath the surface,
I know it's still there.

I try again, using my nails this time.
My nails cut into my skin, making crescent moon
shapes on my wound.
I can see the ball bulge, but doesn't budge.
The more it refuses, the more I want it out.

It has to come out, nothing else matters.
I grab a needle, and pinch the spot.
The ball comes just a bit closer to the surface.
Perfect.
I take the needle, and stab it into the bulge.
I squeeze again, and still nothing comes out.
The needle again, a little further this time.
Maybe making a couple little circles will help.

A half hour has passed, and still I'm fixated.
On this imperfection, which refuses to be
eliminated.
What once was a tiny spot, is now an open sore.
It continues to grow the more I pick,
but it doesn't matter.
When the imperfection is removed, I'll stop.

I'm starting to lose interest, I can no longer tell
what's what.
Just a bloody mess, a huge sore spot.
I'll come back to it, I always do.
I find another spot in the meantime.

I know what I'm doing, I really do.
I try hard to stop, but I always go back.
Sometimes I don't even notice I'm doing it,
until I look down at my fingers,
and see blood on my fingertips,
and the hole left behind.
I have favorite spots I seem to gravitate to.
There's scars all over my body, but not that
anyone sees,
I dress in a manner that usually hides it.

All I want to do is be perfect,
and these spots aren't perfect.
I look at my body,
gnarly, bloody, infected scabs cover my skin.
I know there's something under them.
And I start to pick again.

Curiosity

I'm so bored.
Mommy's at work, and daddy's playing video
games.
My brother and sister are picking on each other,
and I have no one to play with.
I'm gonna look for something to play with.

Hmm, I know what this is!
Mommy and daddy use it to open toys
sometimes.
My big brother too.
I wonder if I can open one of mine.
I climb off of the chair,
screwdriver in hand,
and make my way down the hall
to my room.

I've seen it done before,
I'm a big girl, I can do it too.
I just need to find a toy to unscrew.
I sift through my toys;
this one's too small,
this one's already empty.
Oh look!
I found one!

I put the toy in my tiny lap,
carefully line the screwdriver in the screw,
and start to spin.
At first, nothing happens.
It makes a weird sound and pops up a little.
Let's try the other way.
Oh look! It's moving now!
I spin it and spin it until the screw falls out,
and I pick at the lid until it lifts.

Hmm.. I haven't seen these batteries before.
Three tiny, shiny, flat circles.
I pick them out with my tiny fingers,
it's a good thing I'm so small!
I pinch two of them together with my fingers;
I like the way they slide around,
I wonder if it feels the same in my mouth.
I pop the batteries in my mouth,
the smooth texture on my tongue is entertaining.

I pinch them together between my teeth this
time.
Hey, I can do it with my mouth too!
I move my jaw side to side to make them slide.
One of them slips,
and gulp,
down my throat.
I spit the other one out in my hand.

Uh oh, daddy just saw me spit it out.
He yells and holds out his hand,
I give him the tiny circle.
"Is that all of them?" he asks.
I nod my head, "Yes, daddy."
I can't give him the one in my tummy.

I play with my brother and sister,
I've completely forgotten what happened earlier.
My tummy is starting to hurt.
"I don't feel so good," I tell them.
"Have you eaten?" my brother asks.
"Have you had some water? Mom says your
tummy
can hurt if you haven't had enough," she sister
chimes in.
She gets me some water,
my brother gets me food.
I start to drink,
and the yucky feeling gets worse.
I don't know what's happening,
and I start to puke.

"Looks like you've got a stomach flu,"
daddy says to me.
But no matter what he does,
I still feel yucky.
I puke again, there's so much pain,

"My tummy hurts daddy."
"I know sweetie," then he's gone again.

Mommy comes home and comes to see me.
"Something's wrong," she says,
"This isn't a flu. How long has she been like
this?"
Mommy and daddy start fighting,
trying to figure out what's happening.
I'm so tired, the pain is exhausting.
I close my eyes and fall asleep.

When I wake up, I'm not in my room.
Mommy's crying, and daddy's walking away.
A doctor hugs mommy, and tells her it's not her
fault;
that things like this happen, it's not anyone's
fault.
I try to touch mommy, but my hand goes right
through.
Why can't I touch her?
I just want to give her a hug too.

Breathing

A drop falls on my face, it's starting to rain.
I seek cover under the bus shelter.
It's evening, the sun is fading;
all I want to do is go home.
But I'm patient, and live in the moment,
so I take a deep, rain-scented breath.
The smell has always been my favorite.

I watch the streetlights wake up,
and shine on the wet roads and pavement.
I watch the reflections change shape and color,
and listen to the sound of the falling rain,
the wet tires rolling by, and...
breathing?
The hair on my neck stands up, suddenly I
realize:
I don't know how long
the breathing has been there, behind me.
My whole body tenses, I'm too afraid to look
behind me.

My instinct takes over, and I start running.
I don't know where I'm going, only that it's
far away from here.

I glance over my shoulder, and glimpse a dark
shadow.
My heart starts to pound as I run faster,
it's following me.
I can still hear the breathing,
even over the sound of my own.

I try hard not to slip on the wet pavement,
I start to panic.
"Somebody help me!" I scream,
the pedestrians stare or ignore me.
I turn left, around the corner,
and try even harder to run a bit faster.
I hear gurgling and growling
coming from behind me,
and I let out a scream.

My heart feels like it's in my throat,
my body white hot with adrenaline.
I've lost touch with all other sensation.
I can't hardly breathe, my chest is so tight,
but still I run with all of my might.
One of the panels in the sidewalk,
is a touch too high, and I trip, and fall.

I scramble to get to my feet;
my violent shaking is preventing me
from gaining traction on the sanded sidewalk.
My hands, knees, and feet slip beneath me,

and now,
I'm screaming.
It's coming to get me, and I can't get up.
I feel a hand on my shoulder,
and let out a shriek.
When I turn to look,
I see it's an officer.

Now I sit in the precinct,
still fighting my instinct,
to run away and hide.
"Something was following me," I say again.
"The shadow, you mean?" the officer stares at
me,
and turns a computer screen around
for me to see.
"We've gone over the footage on the street cams.
There's nothing there.
We see you, but not this thing or person
chasing you."
I stare in disbelief, "Show me."

The officer presses play and watches me
intently.
I watch myself a few times, just to be sure.
And each time I'm fleeing, screaming, alone.
Was there really,
nothing behind me?

Stalker

I've been watching you, everything you do.
Your aMiable face makes me believe,
we're simply meant to be.
And yes, alBeit, you don't know me yet;
you will,
and you won't regret it.
You're not a fleEting fancy;
the thought of you consumes
every second of my time.
I have a favorite bencH,
from where I watch you work;
that's how I knew where to leave this letter.
Once I see you leave, I tail you back home.
You sure do walk a lot, Never changing
your routine.
The desire for you is tormenting,
I'm absorbeD in my fantasies,
of what I'd do with you.
But now I'm taking action;
I'm inviting you, cordiallY,
to recognize me as your one and only.
And if you don't want things to get messy,
cooperatiOn is completely necessary;
I take what I want, and what I want is you.

You will take my offer, you can't refuse,
lest my contemptuoUs nature will show through.
25

The Painting

A blank canvas stares back at me,
what will it be this time?
My art is my heart and soul;
each painting I pour myself into.
I pick up my brush, heavy with white,
and start to paint.

Daydreaming about the possibilities
of what the painting could be,
my eyes see the brush moving,
but my mind's eye sees otherwise.
The images morph and change before me,
so many ideas are flowing.

A loud noise startles me out of my daydream,
and I get up to check what happened.
"Damn cat," I mutter after finding a glass
knocked over on the floor down the hallway.
I wander around for a while as I wait for
the base coat to dry.

Upon returning, there is a black spot on the
canvas.

I tilt my head to the side, unsure of how I
remember
leaving the painting.
I could swear I only used white..
No matter, I'm used to pivoting,
as art often requires you to.

I start to block in the areas,
a grove of trees here, a little creek there,
some patches of grass everywhere.
I start adding flowers of all colors,
then the phone begins to ring.
Annoyed, I get up and go to answer the phone.

Sitting down in front of my canvas again,
I pick my brush back up,
and notice the flowers and grass
within a circle, appear to have died
in my painting.
I squint my eyes at the dead spot for a moment,
then go on with covering it up with more paint.

Hours go by, and when I feel like I've finished.
I put the brush down.
Before long, a loud yawn escapes,
and I prepare myself for bed.
This garden scene is absolutely magnificent,
I tell myself as I climb into bed.

Another loud crash makes me bolt upright,
it's much louder this time.
I rub my eyes and look around;
everything seems in order.
Except my canvas, it's face down on the floor.
I climb out of bed, then pick up the canvas.

I gasp as I look at my painting;
all the greenery has died,
the black spot has reappeared,
a trail of footprints and handprints
suggest it came from the spot..

I look down at my floor;
the same set of prints
are now going under my bed.
My heart stops, my blood freezes,
I can't even gasp for air.

A low, croaking growl breaks the silence.

Hiking

Crunch, crunch, crunch;
the gravel sounds beneath me.
The mountain air is crisp.
I've never been here before,
but I think I really like it.
The trail is winding,
trees all around me,
the sound of water running
not too far away.

The aspens are just starting to change,
I pull my camera out and take a picture.

Crunchcrunchcrunchcrunch,
the sound comes up from behind me;
"Can you help me? My friend is hurt!"
I turn to look at the girl,
her hands are bloody,
shaking.
I blink in horror for a moment,
"How can I help?"
"I'm not strong enough to carry her,
if you can carry her to our car,
I can get her to the hospital."

I run after the girl,
it's not long before we're off the trail.
Faster and faster, over logs,
over rocks;
she's getting ahead of me,
what were they doing over here?
I've lost mental track of the map in my head,
so many twists,
so many turns,
nothing but a brown and green blur.
"Hold on, wait for me," I say.
She just keeps going,
rounds a corner,
and is gone.

I stop and scratch my head;
she was here a second ago,
could she really have gone that far,
that fast?
I sit and catch my breath on a log nearby.
Everything's the same,
nothing but identical trees,
all around me.

"Over here, come quick!" her voice calls out.
"Where are you?" I call back,
trying to follow her voice.
"Here! Hurry!" she cries.
I rush in her general direction,

and trip over something on the ground.
I hit so hard, it puts me in a bit of a daze;
this must be what they meant by seeing stars.

I look to see what I tripped over;
a large, moss covered mass is jutting
out of the ground.
Wiggling and pulling, I free it,
and discover,
it's a bone.
I immediately drop it, but still,
too late.
Something stirs below the surface,
and suddenly,
a hand pierces out of the dirt,
and grabs one of my ankles.

Desperately, I try to release the hand.
Another one bursts forth and claims the other
ankle.
I turn on my belly to crawl away,
but it's not working.
They are pulling me into the dirt.
I claw with my hands,
but the dirt just crumbles.
A loud snap comes from my legs,
and I clamp my eyes shut from the pain.

Click

When I open my eyes, I'm back on the trail,
camera in hand.
Was that all just a weird lucid dream?
Perhaps an intense day dream?
I take a big breath in and out.

Then, suddenly, from behind me;
crunchcrunchcrunchcrunch.

Thin Air

Case file: Missing Persons Report
Date: 7/3/22
Name: Clara Robinson
Age: 26
Brown hair, green eyes, approximately 5'6"

Description:
Clara Robinson was reported missing,
after failing to show for a family event.
On the side of a famous stretch of highway,
"The Big Lonely"
is where her vehicle was found.
Security footage from her apartment complex,
shows Clara left around 8:25 am,
and is seen walking to and entering her vehicle.
The same footage shows a hooded figure
watching her leave,
and left shortly after she did,
following the same direction.
The footage was too grainy to identify the
potential suspect.

Street cams confirm Clara's license plate;
her car is seen entering the highway
around 9 am.

Around 10:15 am,
Clara is pulled over and given a warning,
one of her tail-lights isn't working.
Dashcam confirms Clara is released
about 15 minutes after being pulled over.
The officer on duty reports,
the incident was rather routine,
and nothing seemed out of the ordinary.
Upon further review of the footage,
the same hooded figure from before,
is seen by her car as the officer returns to his
vehicle;
the officer reported Clara was alone,
there were no other persons on the scene,
or in her vehicle.
Again, the figure could not be identified,
as no defining features could be made out in the
footage.

This was the last time anyone had seen Clara,
since leaving her apartment.

7/5/22
Clara's mother calls police;
Clara had not made it to her family function,
all calls went unanswered.
More than 24 hours have passed since Clara
left her apartment.
All attempts to contact her were unsuccessful,

which the family reports as being
extremely unusual behavior for Clara.
The family is asked if anyone meant
harm to her;
the family responded that Clara was well loved,
they didn't know of anyone
who would want to cause her harm.

7/9/22
An abandoned vehicle is reported
near the Lovelock exit.
Upon arrival, police confirm the car belongs to
Clara,
the driver door was open.
Her bags, wallet, and personal items are present,
though evidence suggests her car had been
rummaged.
Police managed to pull fingerprints,
but all failed to match any in the database.
3 separate sets of fingerprints were pulled,
one was identified as Clara's.
Blood was also pulled from the scene;
lab tests reveal the blood belonged to Clara.
However, no signs of a struggle or foul-play
were present.
Police investigated the area around her car;
one single footprint was identified and logged.
Forensic analysis shows the footprint did not
match Clara's size or shape.

Police open a full investigation,
and employ the use of the canine unit.

Over 700 hours of canine and volunteer
searches,
all lead to a dead end.
The case went cold.
The case was handed off to the FBI,
and assigned to The Big Lonely task force.
Where did Clara go?
Did the mysterious figure in the footage,
have something to do with her disappearance?

How does someone vanish into thin air?

Butter

Mommy says it's time for bed.
We brush our hair and teeth together,
then I climb up to the top bunk,
and under my blankets.
Mommy has to climb a couple steps,
but still hugs and kisses me goodnight.
Daddy is tall enough though,
he kisses and hugs me too.
They say goodnight to my sister,
and brother in the other room.

I look at my giant bear,
sitting at the foot of my bed.
He's a cream colored bear,
with a cream colored bow;
his black eyes stare blankly back at me,
something seems off.
"Goodnight Butter," I say to him,
then lay down and go to sleep.

I sleep for a while, but,
I mostly toss and turn.
I'm having a hard time staying asleep,
and I'm not sure why.
Sitting up in bed, I rub my eyes.

The faint light from my nightlight
illuminates the entire room.
I'm thankful it's gentle on my eyes.
Butter is still at the foot of my bed,
slumped to one side,
still staring at me with his beady eyes
and little smile.

I go to climb down the ladder,
when I notice him move.
I stop dead in my tracks,
I feel frozen.
Did he really just move?
I slowly curl into a ball at the opposite end,
eyes never leaving my bear.

Then, Butter starts to stand up.
I scream and want to run away,
but I can't move.
He comes towards me, and I start to cry,
and shake.
Butter grabs me, throws me over his shoulder,
and climbs down the ladder.
I kick and scream,
but hitting his plushie body does nothing.

Butter walks towards the window and opens it.
"MOM!! MOMMY!! HELP ME!!"
I scream.

Butter carries me out the window,
and into the night.

39

The Key

My parents used to say,
"This house,
it's been in our family for generations.
And one day, it'll be yours too."
All too soon, that day came,
it was the first item on the inheritance.
One day, I decided to rummage through
boxes in the attic.
I thought I might find something interesting,
in all those dusty old antiques.
All I'd found where books, magazines,
photo albums,
all sorts of average, everyday items.

At the bottom of this particular box,
however,
I found a key;
a beautiful, ornate, skeleton key,
decorated with silver and gold
filigree.
I thought I remembered those details,
from elsewhere.
I took the key with me around the house,
as I tried to find where it belonged.

Something nagged at the back of my mind;
a memory when I was a child,
I was with my grandfather.
He was hunched over,
showing me the same key,
"This key unlocks a very special door.
When you're old enough, and you miss me,
open this door, and we'll be together again.
Just don't spend too much time there,
all good things must come to an end,
lest they become twisted and warped."

The answer dawned on me;
my grandparents suite.

Up the stairs, down the hall,
around the corner, and to the left;
the double doors to my grandparents' suite.
I entered the room and looked around,
I was almost certain the door was behind a
curtain.
One by one, I investigated the curtains;
the one behind the headboard,
I found a lever there.
I pulled the lever, and beside me,
a wall panel rose up,
and revealed an ornate door.

I started to shake as I put the key in the lock;

I had no idea what was on the other side.
Did I really want to know what was there?
Sheer curiosity overtook me,
I turned the lock, then entered.

Inside, there was no floor,
but it behaved like there was.
I stepped into the nothing,
and the door shut behind me.
All around me lit up with memories of my
grandfather,
my grandmother,
mother and father.
I walked toward a memory of my mother,
grandmother, and I making cookies.
Everyone looked so much younger back then.
I remembered it as it played,
and happy tears ran down my face.
I'm so lonely now,
without all my family,
I would give anything to have them back.

I traveled between memories,
some were amazing, others made me cringe.
I decided to revisit some memories,
and started making my way back.
I looked upon a previous memory again,
but something was wrong.
The background appeared melted,

the faces replaced with white splotches.

"Where is the door? I have to get out of here,"
I told myself.
I looked around, but there were no doors in
sight.
Only memories;
they appeared to melt into one another.
I could feel myself starting to quickly forget
where I was,
how I got there,
where I was going.
I kept getting distracted by the swirls;
a great nothingness started to grow in my head.
I watched all the color drain away,
all emotion along with it;
everything around me turned white.

An eternity later,
a door appeared in the distance.
Something.. familiar, tinged inside of me.
I hardly remember my feet moving,
carrying me to the door.
I only remember the door getting bigger,
then it opened in front of me,
and he walked through.

"Do you know who I am?" the doctor asked.

Good Boy

Charleston is there for me whenever I need him.
I come home, he's waiting for me.
I have to go run some errands, he's coming with
me.
Up to the lake?
No one else is more eager than my boy,
he never says no.
And I love him, I can't help myself.
Today, we're visiting the ranch,
his favorite place.

After a few hours in my truck, we finally arrive.
I love going up the mountain;
it's people I don't like.
"Come on Charleston, let's go
say hello
to the old man and his lady," I say as I open the
door for him.
He jumps out, and follows me down the path.

After our visit, I grab my pole and my box,
and head down to the lake.
My boy's not far behind me,
he's taking his time smelling the flowers
and winding between the trees.

He's good about occupying himself while I fish.
I cast my line, and wait.

Several hours go by, and I've caught
a good share of fish.
Something in me tells me to keep going,
it wants to catch
the biggest fish possible.
I cast my line one more time, and wait.

The pole nearly flies into the water,
but my hands are just slightly faster.
I catch the pole midair,
and grip it tight.
Whatever it is is going to give me quite a fight.
Back and forth, side to side,
this one doesn't want to give up.
I reel with all my might, and finally win the
battle.
A strange, gooey looking fish breaches the
surface.

Charleston immediately runs to my side,
and starts to sniff it urgently.
Suddenly, he bites down on it,
and runs into the woods.
Everything happens so quickly,
I have no time to react.
I run after him, hoping to find him

before something bad happens.

Several hours later,
Charleston is nowhere to be found.
I'm worried sick about him,
he's never done anything like this before.
I pace back and forth in the guest cabin.
Suddenly, there's a sound;
it sounds like whining, like an animal is hurt.
I look out the window,
and there's Charleston.
I immediately run out the door to see
my boy.

But... something's not right.
He has patches of wet, gooey fur,
his breathing is labored,
he looks like he doesn't know where he is.
"Hey Charleston, it's me little buddy,"
I reach out for him.
He growls and snaps at me in response,
and starts to walk towards me as he snarls.
"Charleston, stop!" I shout, his growling just
gets louder.
I turn and run for the door,
he starts barking after me.
I manage to shut the door,
but Charleston charges into it.

And manages to break through.

Surprised, I throw myself back,
and am crawling backwards on the floor.
Charleston, baring his teeth in a sinister manner,
slowly steps in.
"Charleston, it's me. It's daddy.
You don't want to hurt daddy,
I know you,
you're my good boy," I plead with him.

Then, Charleston lunges after me.

In the Crack

I've been seeing something,
in the crack.
An eyeball stares back at me
through the crack.
It used to only happen at night,
with my bedroom door.
Whenever I see it, I can't look away.
I'm too scared,
why is it watching me through the crack?

Lately, it's been showing up in other places.
The door to my closet,
the one to my garage.
It's so bad I see it in the cracks of doors
in public.
Sometimes I let out a little shriek,
often I'm caught by surprise.
People stop and stare at me.

Why me?
What does it want from me?
I can hardly close my eyes anymore,
lest I see the eyeball peeking back at me,
through the cracks of my own eyelids.

Sister

Dear Sister,
can you help me?
I'm someone else inside.
The other me tells me horrible things,
unspeakable things.
Everyone tells me it's the devil,
whispering in my ear,
trying to get me to sin,
to give in to temptation,
that it's normal for followers to feel tested.
But I don't feel tested, Sister.
There is someone else inside.

I know it.

It moves in my head,
constantly competing for space.
I'm exhausted, Sister.
It tells me things I wouldn't,
and shouldn't, know.
An example?
Ok..

It says you'll never be a real nun,

you can't hide what you do with the old man
at the altar every Wednesday night.
And that boy you ran over?
You pretend you didn't flee the scene of the
crime.
It says his parents still cry,
because the case is unsolved,
and here you are, in all your piousness.

What's that?
An exorcism?
Oh no, that won't be necessary.

Haiku Horror

51

The children are laughing loudly,
I can hear them from my room;
I don't have any children.

The Hair

52

Something's been tickling me,
I can feel it when I move my arm.
But when I go to grab it,
suddenly it's not there.
As soon as my arm's back down,
it's tickling me again.

I scratch and tug,
pick and pluck,
and once I get lucky, I give it a tug.
I pull and pull, trading hands as I'm pulling.
This hair's so long,
when is it ending?
My feet start to tickle,
and kind of feel funny.
But I'm still pulling.

There's so much hair, it looks like
I pulled out a lock of my own.
I'm getting alarmed,
where is this hair coming from?
I set it down and try to stand up,
but I can't.
My pants look deflated,
my legs have gone missing.

Catfish

Another date gone wrong,
sometimes I wonder why I even bother.
Sometimes I look at these people,
and wonder,
am I that desperate too?

Brring

My notification sound, it's a text from my friend.
No one's seen him since he matched up with
this girl on the Mingle app, what does he want?

>I know you've been putting yourself out there,
but definitely give this app a try!
You won't regret it, promise!

I let out a loud sigh.
Alright, you win.
I guess I am that desperate,
I think to myself.
I tap on the link.
Eh, the site doesn't look bad, I suppose.
I create an account, and upload a picture.

Bedeep

A new notification sound,
looks like they have matches for me to browse.
I feel like I'm shopping for a partner;
"you ARE shopping for a partner, idiot,"
my internal dialogue responds.
"Shut the fuck up," I say to myself under my
breath.
I thumb through some of the matches,
but none really strike me.

Bedeep

>You have one new message!

Huh, probably a robot, but I'm curious,
so I open it.

Rena Hudson
35/f/Denver

>Hey there. I see you're also in Denver;
I'm new here and really just want to connect
with someone.
I have a pretty open schedule if you want to
meet up sometime.

I tap on her picture,
her hair is half red, half black.

She has a pouty expression on her face.
I decide to write her back:
"Hello, yes I am in Denver. I'll have to get back
to you,
my schedule hasn't been released yet.
But maybe we could video chat in the
meantime?"

A few minutes go by,
I'm anxious to get back home.
It's been a long night,
and I could use the rest.

Bedeep brring, bedeep brring

Rena is calling you!

I tap the green phone button.
"Hello?"
All I hear is static.
"Hello? Rena, are you there?"
Bits and pieces of words escape through the
static.
"I can't hear you," I say loudly,
I can barely hear myself over the noise.

"I can hear you," a woman's voice clearly says.
Hands spring forth from my screen and drag me
in.

Favorite Song

I've been waiting for a new set of headphones,
nothing seems to satisfy me.
My ear canals are small,
and earbuds are too big and uncomfortable.
I don't like wrap-around headphones either,
too clunky, chunky,
and they pull my hair out.

But these headphones, these are special order.
I had impressions made of my inner ears,
so these will fit me, only me,
and no one else.
They arrived today, and they've been charging,
it's almost time to test them out.
I disconnect them from the charger,
and pair them with my phone.
I get my favorite song ready,
and place the buds in my ears.

The song starts to play, and it feels like heaven.
The sound quality is so good, I feel like
the band is playing in front of me,
only for me.
I start to get emotional, and tears fall down my
face.

This song gets me every time.
I wipe my face and look down at my hands.

Blood?
Where is this coming from?
I wipe my eyes again, more blood.
I try to take the headphones off,
but fail.
My head starts to ring and pound,
my eyes feel like they're going to pop.
Blood is coming out of my eyes and ears now.
The pain is so excruciating,
all I can do is hold my head,
and collapse onto my knees.

The sound gets sharper, the pitch gets higher,
then everything goes black.

The End

"Life is what you make it," I hear Karen say.
Well Karen, please go fuck yourself.
You were born with a silver spoon in your
mouth,
and have never wanted for anything,
a day in your life.
I don't want to hear your words of
toxic positivity,
your "Live, Laugh, Love."
I want a reason to live.
A real reason to keep going.
I want to feel validated for my experiences,
to be told
I didn't deserve what happened to me.

To feel like I matter,
to not be in so much emotional turmoil all the
time.
To be at peace within myself,
to have a passion for being alive.
None of these things are present.
Can I Live, Laugh, Love my way into
happiness?
Or will you turn me on to god?
Because "through god all things are possible.

You were put through that because
he knew you were strong enough."
Why do I have to be tested to prove,
I am worthy of love?
Why do I have to prove I am strong enough?
Am I not supposed to be loved when I am weak,
and need it most?
Should I be ashamed of wanting attention?

Everything's been weighing heavily on me;
the state of the world, the state of my mind,
the hopelessness of not being able to change
anything.
What's the point?
Lately, the thought gets sweeter
every day.
The Call of the Void is singing my name,
and it feels like home.
I don't belong here anymore,
I don't think I ever did.
I've always felt alone,
no matter who surrounded me.

I laugh, and I smile,
but all the while,
I'm thinking about how I want
the embrace of
the end.